KATH

HEP

LITTL ME

PENGUIN BOOKS

PENGUIN BOOKS

Published by the Penguin Group. Penguin Books Ltd, 27 Wrights Lane, London W8 5TZ, England. Penguin Books USA Inc., 375 Hudson Street, New York, New York 10014, USA. Penguin Books Australia Ltd, Ringwood, Victoria, Australia. Penguin Books Canada Ltd, 10 Alcorn Avenue, Toronto, Ontario, Canada M4V 3B2. Penguin Books (NZ) Ltd, 182–190 Wairau Road, Auckland 10, New Zealand · Penguin Books Ltd, Registered Offices: Harmondsworth, Middlesex, England · These extracts are from *Me* by Katharine Hepburn, first published in the USA by Alfred A. Knopf, Inc., New York 1991. Published simultaneously in Canada by Random House of Canada Ltd, Toronto. First published in Great Britain by Viking 1991. Published in Penguin Books 1992. This edition published 1996. · Typeset by Rowland Phototypesetting Ltd, Bury St Edmunds, Suffolk. Printed in England by Clays Ltd, St Ives plc · · 10 9 8 7 6 5 4 3 2 1

CONTENTS

Hartford

So, I was born eighty-odd years ago, May 12, 1907, despite everything I may have said to the contrary. In Hartford, Connecticut – 22 Hudson Street – then opposite the Hartford Hospital. The street doesn't exist anymore. The hospital grew over it. Dad had finished his internship and was no longer forced to live in the hospital itself.

Hartford is the capital of Connecticut. It is a charming city full of parks and hills and even elm trees – some lovely old houses – good skating and skiing in winter – hot in summer.

Very soon after my birth, we moved to 133 Hawthorn Street. It had a fireplace with 'Listen to the Song of Life' scrolled across the top. It was a lovely early-Victorian house with three peaks – the center one bigger. Red brick painted with a black lace trim. It doesn't exist anymore either. It was next to the Arrow Electric Factory, east of us. Next to the corner of Forest, to the west of us, some people named Bennett built a house right on the corner.

They had a cement tennis court and became close friends. We had the remains of a clay court at the south end of our property. Ours was a long and fairly wide piece of land with a stream along the factory side at the bottom of a sort of little woodland of trees – mostly hemlock and pine. At the front of the property the driveway was a big circle to the front door. The house was about seventy feet from the street. In the winter when there was a heavy snow, we'd enclose the circle in a high wall of snow, very thick. Terrible battles would ensue. It was like a feudal town.

The lawn was deep and ran back to the railroad track. Brownie Park was next to the track. Now it's all part of the highway. There was a lovely pond in Brownie Park. It was full of rats. I think rats can swim. We had a raft on it. A hedge of Paul's scarlet roses bordered the property on the west. To the east there was a gulch with a lot of trees so that we couldn't see the factory – a sort of woods full of daffodils and jack-in-the-pulpits and trillium. What a charming place! There was the railroad track – then Brownie Park – then a cedar hedge – then the remains of a tennis court – then another bit of wood – then the lawn – then the house.

To the east of the circle was a group of big trees. Some were cut down to make tables or chairs. We used to have tea there in the spring. It was pretty. It was fun.

People, friends in the neighborhood would drift in. Tea was a favorite gathering time.

There was a hemlock tree on the west side of the property. That was the tree I used to climb. The neighbors used to call Mother.

'Kit! Kathy is in the top of the hemlock!'

'Yes, I know. Don't scare her. She doesn't know that it's dangerous.'

There was another tree, an elm, which played a big part in our lives. Just to the west of the driveway and about fifty feet in from the street. It had a tall trunk and went up straight without any branches. About sixty feet up there was a strong branch growing straight out almost parallel to the ground. To this branch Dad tied a swinging ladder. We would climb up this long wooden ladder to get to a trapeze on a pulley, which was all set to ride a rope which went from the elm to the very back of our long property. We'd get onto the trapeze sitting or hanging by our knees and ride down the rope, which of course started high up and went down to ground level. It was thrilling! Across the gravel path, down to our back door, across the back lawn and to the end.

It used to terrify people. Dad was a very good athlete. He wanted us to be too – if we lived. Mother not being an athletic type would suffer as she saw her daughter riding the trapeze over the gravel walk hanging by her feet so high in the air. But she kept silent. She thought it looked fun.

On Sundays and holidays we'd walk in the woods. We'd climb. We'd swing trees, climb up as high as we could – then, holding on as tight as possible, we'd swing our legs out and bend the treetop over to the ground. Birches were best. They are very bendable. It was exciting.

It was great fun. Because of Dad we were the center of action. And because of Mother we were always able to provide cookies and ginger ale or sarsaparilla or birch beer. But the greatest gift she gave us was *freedom* to be noisy, to yell. No nags. Do it? Yes, do it! And tell me about it.

Dad, as I've said, had an old Maxwell car. The license was 3405. He used to come home early from the office in the afternoon, at four-thirty. He was determined to know his own kids. All the children in the neighborhood would be collected in our yard waiting for him. We all loved him.

We'd shout, '3405!' as he came into view – '3405!' Into the driveway he'd come. He'd change his clothes – have a cup of tea with Mother – then for the next hour we'd play baseball or prisoner's base. We'd play on our court or on the Bennetts' court.

Can you imagine that Dr Thomas N. Hepburn, my father, used to drag us on sleds behind his car through the streets of Hartford, Connecticut, after a snowstorm – Hawthorn to Forest out Farmington to Woodland to Asylum to Elizabeth Park? Or straight out Woodland to Keney Park. A long rope played out off the backseat. All cars were open – at least I believe so. Anyone who wanted to could hook on. Anyone who could would stay on. Dad would try to sling us off speeding around every corner. He never got rid of me. Great fun.

I remember once it was my birthday and I thought, Well now, my birthday! I can choose prisoner's base. I liked it much better than baseball.

'Prisoner's base,' I said.

'Oh no, baseball!' they all cried.

'But, Dad – it's my birthday – certainly I have the right to –'

'You have the privilege of making everyone happy,' said Dad. 'It's your birthday.'

We played baseball. Unfair!

Another incident, sort of similar. When we were much younger, about eight.

At birthday parties we used to have a pin-the-tail-on-the-donkey contest. We'd hang a piece of material with the donkey drawn out – a full-sized donkey. The guests would be blindfolded and given a tail to pin on the donkey.

On my birthday I did a bit of advance work. I knew where the donkey would be hung. I studied the rug edges which I could feel through my shoes – then nine steps – reach to the left – tail-high.

When at the party I pinned the tail almost exactly where it belonged, Mother cheerily said, 'Well, that was excellent. You –'

'I won! I won!' I said.

'Oh no,' said Mother. 'You can't win anything. It's your party. You *give* the prizes.'

Pretty dumb, I thought to myself. Life! Dumb!

Tom's and my first nurse was Lizzie Byles. She was married to Cecil Byles. She was very English and

 the whole setup was very very correct. Then when

Mother got interested in suffrage and they opened the headquarters at 22 Pratt Street, Lizzie was asked down there. She could type. Goodbye, nurse.

I must say that during all this time we'd had a cook – Fanny Ciarrier – and her son Marcel, who was my age and who always lived with us. She was an Italian-French woman who was blind in one eye. She could cook anything and everything. If we needed a maid – a nurse – a whatever, Fanny would import them from Italy or France. She was an angel and was with us all our lives. And when Fanny died, Mother soon followed her.

Fanny's brother was a chef at the Hartford Club.

Dad and Mother had answered an ad to find her. She had had herself listed as available for service – a want ad. Dad had a theory that if you want to hire help, go to their home to see how they live. So Dad and Mother went to meet her. In the middle of the meeting, the room was very stuffy. Fanny got up and opened a window. She's right, thought Dad, the air is stale. He hired her. Forever. Lucky us. She was sensitive.

I learned to ride a bike in Keney Park. I was three. It had been especially made at the Pope Manufacturing Company. Dad put me on and started me downhill. Terrified I was. Far in the distance was a little old man. He was slowly moving along at the bottom of the hill – the only figure in view. As if he were a magnet, I headed for him and I finally managed to bump him. But he'd seen kids on new bikes before. He was waiting for me.

Anyway, I learned quickly. It wasn't long before they would telephone Mother: 'Your little girl Kathy has just been seen on her bike on Farmington past Sigourney heading downtown.'

'Yes,' said Mother. 'Thank you.'

I had a horse run away with me too in Keney Park. There was a family named Anninger. They used to rent horses at Troop B Armory on Farmington just past Quaker Lane. When I was in Oxford School – the girls' private school in Hartford – we had a riding class there. Sergeant Anninger used to put me on a pony named Leopard. He was speckled and I was speckled and I loved him dearly. So the years passed. I became famous and I went one day to Sergeant Anninger to rent a horse. He'd moved his stable to Keney Park. He apparently thought my riding had progressed along with my fortunes, so he put me on his special mount. Off we went – my sisters Marion and Peg and I – a wild ride tearing under branches over hills over streams. I am ashamed to say I 'gripped leather.' But I lived.

'Well, Kathy, how did you do?' . . . Dear Sergeant Anninger.

'I did fine. I'm here – ain't I?'

I went to West Middle School when I was a kid – four. A public school. Kindergarten and then on up to fifth grade. I walked east on Hawthorn, north on Laurel, across Farmington to Niles, a step right and there it was on my left. About a mile in all. I headed a group of kids who wanted Police Officer O'Malley to remain at the Farmington Avenue and Laurel Street crosswalk. They had decided to move him to a different location. He was fun. We petitioned and won. O'Malley stayed.

At the east end of Niles Street was Trinity Church. The daughter of the pastor was my great friend – Florence Miele. She was pretty – gorgeous curly brown hair – long. I was freckled – wore my hair like a boy's. In fact, with one brother Tom older and my two younger, Dick and Bob, being a girl was a torment. I'd always wanted to be a boy. Jimmy was my name, if you want to know.

Anyway, to wonder again as we do today about

the unexplainable things kids do. We were in fifth grade. Our teacher was Miss Lynes. She was thin and tall and severe-looking. But the opposite inside. I was good at arithmetic, which was her specialty. She liked me and I liked her. We'd indicated as much to each other.

One day at lunchtime Florence and I lied to our respective families as to where we were lunching and hid at the school. The teachers all used to have their lunch in a long thin room on the second or third floor – facing Niles. When we were sure the teachers were all eating, Florence (the minister's daughter) and I (the daughter of two very 'state-of-humanity'-conscious parents) rushed out and at the top of our lungs and in vulgar tones screamed: 'Old Lady Lynes! Old Lady Lynes!'

It brought shame to the school, shame to our parents and must really have puzzled Miss Lynes. Mother forced me to carry a potted geranium from Hawthorn Street to school and present it to Miss Lynes – an admission of my guilt and an indication of my sorrow. Miss Lynes put in on her desk. It was there humiliating me for weeks.

And there are so many geraniums in California – reminding me to remember: if you sin you pay.

Miss Lynes forgave me. We were friends for years.

Mother and Jo Bennett (Mrs Toscan Bennett) were great friends and in the forefront of the fight for women's suffrage – for birth control – for recognition of blacks' rights – fighting prostitution. Jo Bennett's mother, Katharine Beach Day, was also a member of the group. She was wealthy – had a car and driver and was Old Hartford and very socially O.K. Another friend was Emily Pierson of Cromwell, Connecticut – daughter of the owner of Cromwell Gardens (a huge conglomeration of greenhouses – wholesale – beautiful roses). Emily had studied medicine and was Dr Pierson. She practiced in Cromwell and was a dyed-in-the-wool reformer.

These were strong women, and not penniless, and socially in the right group, which meant a lot in those days.

Most of the husbands were of the same mind as the women. That was unusual.

Dad had the energy and brain but no money except what he earned. Toscan Bennett had money and local family connections.

Our house at teatime was a meeting ground. We

kids were allowed in but we didn't do much talking – if any. We met Emmeline Pankhurst, Margaret Sanger, Rebecca West, Richard Bennett – and any number of distinguished doctors and professors.

Dad asked George Bernard Shaw to write the preface to *Damaged Goods* – a French play by Brieux about venereal disease. He had one hundred copies – or was it one thousand? – printed in English at his own expense, and sent them around with a note about the Social Hygiene Association. He asked them to return the price of the book if they were impressed by it. He had a 98-percent acceptance for his effort. Richard Bennett did the play on Broadway. He was the father of Constance and Joan.

I thought about this one day and sorted through some of Dad's letters to try to find his correspondence with Shaw. No luck. He had thrown it away. The important thing to him was that he had done it and that it had been presented to the world in a language which they could understand. Make the world a better place to live in for everyone – especially the underprivileged. Progress.

There were many people who violently disagreed with what Mother and Dad were aiming at. As I told you, we were snubbed by the reactionaries and became quite used to it. Whatever the opposition does, take it with a grain of salt. Smile. You don't hear or see bad things. Good morning. Thank you. How interesting. Oh, I guess she didn't hear me.

And gradually the majority joined our side. And Mother was right and Dad too of course. And naturally *we* were on the right side too. And it was all for the benefit of the helpless – the oppressed – the poor – of course! The things Mother and Dad fought for turned out in their favor.

We felt that our parents were the best two people in the world – that we were wildly lucky to be their children. And we still feel that way.

Often my sister Peg, who runs a farm, will look at me and say, 'Can you imagine? Mother and Dad. Weren't we lucky?'

And my brother Bob, the doctor – he will just gloat about them. And Dick, who is a playwright.

We are all aware of our great good fortune. I think of the things I have enjoyed and have learned.

All the sports – golf, tennis, diving, swimming, running, jumping. Dad was responsible for building a good springboard and diving tower on the pier. Wrestling – mat work – gymnastics at Fenwick. He started the custom of contests – of track meets. Our family won so many firsts that they put a limit on the number of wins for one person.

I love diving. Hell – I love all sports. I was skinny and very strong and utterly fearless. There was a pier at Fenwick and a diving board on the pier. The height of the board from the water naturally varied with the tide. There was a railing on the pier about two and a half or three feet high. In order to get a better spring, I would stand on the top of the railing, jump off it to the end of the board and dive – either a jackknife, a swan dive, a one-and-a-half or a somersault. Running off the end of the board, I would do a half gainer. Standing on the end of the board, a back flip or a back dive. It was fun.

All these complicated dives I did – big show-off ever. One day we had a contest. My great friend Ali Barbour, who – well, she was no athlete – she did a prayer dive. It's just what it sounds. Kneel on the end of the board and fall off.

Well, as I said, we had a fancy diving contest. I assumed that I'd win. I did my half gainer. It's about as unsafe a dive as you can imagine. Run off the end of the board – throw one leg out up in the air – arch the back – let the other leg join the first leg – point the toes – and you dive back toward the board and twist your body into a front dive down into the water. I did it – brilliantly, I thought. Ali did her prayer dive – pathetic, I thought. Ali Barbour won it. Can you imagine? They said that my toes were not quite together and not pointed. Oh my golly. My toes. True disgrace. Beaten by a prayer dive. Can you imagine?

Golf became a sort of specialty with me and with Bob. We went to Fenwick in the summer where there was a private nine-hole course, and as very young kids we could play at any time. Dad was a Deadeye Dick putter. We began at five. When I was twelve or thirteen, Mother started me on lessons at the Hartford Golf Club from an Englishman named Jack Stait. Bob was a natural. We became really quite good. Mother, who had never had any athletic training, struggled with golf and with swimming and diving. She believed in teachers.

During that winter when we lived in Hartford, I decided to tutor instead of going to Oxford School. I wanted to be able to play golf every day. Well, actually I didn't want to be in any school. Too many girls. Too much curiosity. I'll tell you why.

My brother Tom, who was two and a half years older than I, had just died under strange circumstances. I adored him. I was fourteen years old.

Actually, Tom's death has remained unexplained. It was Eastertime. Kingswood – the boys' private school in Hartford – was on holiday. Tom and I were to go to New York to visit Aunt Mary Towle. She had a charming house on Charlton Street in the Village. She had been at Bryn Mawr College with Mother. They had become great friends. Auntie was a lawyer. And the house next door on Charlton was occupied by Bertha Rembaugh. They had been partners. Bertha had become a judge. They were very nice and very successful. Mary Towle never married. We called her Auntie and she was generous and fun. When we visited her, she took us to plays and showed us the sights of the big city.

This visit we went to the theatre to see *A Connecticut Yankee in King Arthur's Court*.

When we got home from the theatre, I can't really tell you what we did. But as I later told the story, I said that Tom had looked at me and said, 'You're my girl, aren't you? You're my favorite girl in the whole world.' Why did I say this? Was it true? I mean, did Tom really say it? I don't know any longer.

At Auntie's, Tom used to sleep in a sort of studio attic at the top of the house. It was full of junk and trunks and had no ceiling – just roof and rafters. His bed was a cot next to the wall.

The facts were as follows. Next morning I went upstairs to wake him up. There he was – next to the bed – his knees bent – hanged by a torn piece of sheeting. It was tied to a rafter. He was dead. Strangled.

It made no sense.

In a state of numb shock I cut him down and laid him on the bed.

Tom was dead. He was just plain dead.

Yes. I touched him. Cold. He was dead.

What should I do? Whom should I tell? Auntie was too emotional – she would be frantic.

A doctor. Get a doctor.

I went downstairs and out the front door. I had seen a doctor sign on one of the houses across the street. I went to the door and rang the bell. It was about eight o'clock in the morning. The door was opened a crack by a woman peering out.

'Yes?'

'My brother's dead.'

A moment's pause.

'What?' she said.

'My brother – he's dead.'

'Then the doctor can't help him, can he?'

'No.'

Bang.

She closed the door. She just closed the door.

I stood for a moment. No – yes, it's too late for the doctor. Yes, she is right. The doctor – too late for the doctor to help. Oh dear – poor Auntie. She'll . . .

I'd better go back.

Now what.

I rang the bell at Aunt Bertha's house. She answered. 'Tom is dead,' I said. Then I burst into tears. This was what I thought I should do. People die – you cry – but inside I was frozen.

Aunt Bertha took over. She told Auntie. They called Mother and Dad. Mother and Dad and Jo Bennett came to New York.

I just remember confusion then. We were on a boat crossing the Hudson with Tom's body, going to a crematorium in New Jersey. I can remember standing with Dad on the bow of the ferry. I looked across at Mother – standing with Jo Bennett – about twenty feet away. She was crying. My mother was crying. Oh dear. What can I do? I'd never seen my mother cry before. And I never saw her cry again. Never. She was stalwart.

She had had her share of serious problems. Her father's suicide. Her mother's death at thirty-four of cancer. She had been sixteen at the time. The responsibility of her two sisters as children twelve and fourteen. If she cried, she cried alone.

My father didn't cry either. He took what life had to offer.

I only saw him once – what shall I say? – thrown for a loop. It was one day in early 1951. Dad and I had gone to Fenwick. We had left Mother in Hartford to take her afternoon nap. We were getting back for tea at five. When we got home, we walked into the living room. No fire in the fireplace. Mother's chair was empty. No fire? We rushed upstairs and opened the bedroom door. Mother was there – dead.

I looked at Dad.

'Oh no – no,' he said. 'I can't – she can't –'

'Go down, Daddy. Go down – don't look –'

Mother had had her nap every day. This was a

must. She was getting dressed for tea. She must have felt something queer. She went from her dressing room into the bedroom, got into bed and with her left hand was pulling the covers up – and bingo – dead.

I stood – my mother – dead – my darling mother – the only mother I'll ever have – gone.

I took her hand – still warm – unclasped her fingers from the sheet she had pulled up – and I kissed her and went down to Dad.

No goodbyes. Just gone.

After Tom's death, she went to the Cedar Hill Cemetery when we buried his ashes, but afterward she never mentioned him. She never said, 'I'm going to the cemetery.' Neither did Dad. They moved on into life.

At first the newspapers said Tom had committed suicide. There was no reason for this that anyone could see.

Then Dad made a statement that it was very possible that Tom was practicing hanging himself. Dad had told us about his trick of pretending to hang as a kid.

In football games or baseball, the teams that came
 from the North were very aware of the Southern

attitude toward the Negro. And felt that the Virginians – Dad was a Virginian – were cruel and felt superior to the blacks. As a means of irritating these Northerners, the Virginians trained several blacks to pretend they were being hanged. Dad was an expert at this. It was holding his neck in a certain position – a trick – that prevented the noose from cutting off his wind.

Dangerous sport. Could it be that Tom was practicing this and using sheeting instead of rope – the noose was slippery and he could not control it? Dad felt this was a reasonable possibility. And how this must have tortured Dad, but we never talked about it.

None of the family or his close friends could imagine why he might do it deliberately.

Jimmy Soby, who went to Kingswood School with Tom, could think of no reason. Tom was tops in the school – a prefect – a great athlete – a fine student – a leader of boys. Why?

There seemed to be a sort of feeling at the time that he might have made a pass at his girl and maybe it didn't work out and maybe in despair he – Anyway, we'll never know.

I thought at first that it wasn't possible that he

was practicing hanging. Now I wonder. Deep in my heart – I wonder.

It's amazing how Dad's and Mother's behavior left its mark. They simply did not believe in moaning about anything.

The important thing was that Tom was dead. In the first terrible shock Mother cried. Yes. But she never allowed the fact of his death to dominate the atmosphere. We were not a sad household.

My sister Peg had a son Tom, who was lost in the Vietnam War. He was missing at first, then pronounced dead. His twin sister was talking about him one day – he was so this, so that – to the other younger children. Peg heard her.

'Don't do that!' she said to her daughter.

'But –' she said.

'No buts,' said Peg. 'He's dead. We all love him but he's gone. Don't moan. It does no good.'

She's right of course.

Anyway, this incident seemed to sort of separate me from the world as I'd known it.

I tried school but it was – well, I should say I was – I felt isolated. I knew something that the girls did not know: tragedy.

 They were curious and I would not, did not,

want to talk or to discuss it. The school year ended at the end of May and I never returned. In the fall I decided to tutor.

Luckily I was tall for my age and I was a good driver, and Mother used to let me take her car to go for my tutoring lessons. Physics, English, French and History. I could do it by bicycle but the car was better. As Dad had the Chief of Police as a patient, the cops were very careful not to see me. Actually, all went well until the day Mother and I went to look at Bryn Mawr. I had driven out to the Hartford Golf Club to get my clubs. I had heard a lot about the Merion Cricket Club, and since it was close to Bryn Mawr I thought I might try it.

As I was coming down Asylum Avenue – a big avenue – at a good clip east of Scarborough, an old man on my right (which fact gave him the right-of-way) shot out of a side street. In order to avoid him, I went over to the wrong side of Asylum. Instead of his turning sharp to avoid me, he too went to the wrong side and we collided. At the same time I knocked over the police telephone. Well, I had also caved in the side of his car. He wasn't hurt. I wasn't hurt. He wept and put his arms around me. I thought, Well, the thing to do is to weep. So I did.

The Chief of Police called Dad: 'Hello, Hep, you've heard about Kath?'

'She collided with an old boy on Asylum. Caved in the side of his car. His fault yes, but she is in the wrong of course.'

'Yes, quite completely. Oh, and Hep, she knocked down a police telephone. And I hate to say this, but the front of your old Reo is also quite badly . . .

'Oh, I think five grand will probably cover everything quite well, Hep.'

Mother and I were on the train to Bryn Mawr.

Happily!

My tutoring years were very pleasant. As I told you, I took daily golf lessons with Jack Stait. It looked as though I were going to develop into a pretty good player. I could hit it a mile. And I was quite accurate with irons. The only thing I just was lousy at was putting. Oh dear. I wonder now if even then my head and/or hands shook. Not so that you could see it but so that when tensed up I was sort of uneasy. Well, whatever it was, I just could not putt. Then – now – ever.

It had been a great relief to me not to have to go to school and not to have to associate with girls. My two really good friends, Ali Barbour and Timmy Robinson, had left Oxford to go to the Ethel Walker School in Simsbury. Being more or less alone didn't bother me. We had a seamstress – Mary Ryan – who used to come every Thursday. I used to talk to her. She was Irish and very nice. Then I also had a little theatre, which I had made out of a wooden box. It had a floor with lines cut in it every half inch – green – parallel to the front. I could stand the scenery and the actors in the cracks. I'd make up the stories.

I also had a curtain, which I could open and close.

I would give shows to my brothers Dick and Bob. They seemed to like it.

Dad used to take us to the movies every Saturday night. There were three theaters we could visit – the Strand, the Majestic, the Empire. The Empire ran Westerns and it was easy to park the car. Silent movies – Tom Mix – William S. Hart. My Western heroes. I adored movies. I still do. What a great medium! Leatrice Joy and Thomas Meighan in *Manslaughter*.

I have to tell the truth. There was a Poli's Theater too, on Main Street. We never went there because there was vaudeville and Dad didn't care for it.

Oh, I remember one funny thing. Mother almost never came with us to the movies. She thought that movies were – silly. Didn't matter. I remember an incident at the Majestic. Because Dad was busy, Mother took us. It was a very sentimental movie but somehow it struck Mother as funny. She laughed quite loud – and she continued to laugh. The usher came down and asked her to leave. I was humiliated. Such a disgrace. You can see Mother just did not find movie stories palatable. She had a very highbrow brain. Curious that Fate gave her a movie-queen daughter.

They used to go to any good play which came to Parson's Theater. If we wanted to go, they would get us matinée seats. Our visits were infrequent. I used to bribe Dick and Bob to go to the corner drugstore to buy me movie magazines. These I found fascinating. At the same time they'd buy themselves and me ice-cream sundaes covered with chocolate sauce and marshmallow and chocolate shot. They were called Chocolate Imperials. The money for these delights I earned in the winter by shoveling snow in our driveway and various sidewalks in the neighborhood. Cutting lawns and leaf raking at other seasons.

The house at 133 Hawthorn, which Mother and Dad had occupied from early on, was to be torn down and the Arrow Electric was to extend its building to fill the 133 property.

Dad, with four children and another on the way, could not wait to find a place. He found 352 Laurel Street. Not anywhere near as nice as 133 but the best available at that time. He had altered 352 quite considerably and at quite an expense. We were ready to move when the Forest Street Association bought 133 as a historic building. They immediately called Mother. She called Dad and urged him to stay in 133. But Dad was adamant and refused. Said he'd leased 352 for two years and that was that. So we moved.

Mother had adored 133 Hawthorn. The house and property had real charm and distinction. She had been heartbroken at the thought of 352 Laurel. I thought Mother was right: 133 was unique and beautiful; 352 was really nothing much. Poor Mother. She never forgot it. And I remember thinking, When you have a choice like that, you must be very careful not to just go down a road because you had planned to. If you have a choice, be careful to be influenced only by what is best in the long run.

We weren't rich and Dad was thinking of the wasted money.

We lived at 352 and we bought a piece of property at 201 Bloomfield Avenue, opposite Hartford University. There we began to plan the perfect house.

Tom and I were born at 22 Hudson.

Dick and Bob were born at 133.

Marion and Peg at 352.

Now here I am in Hartford on one of those frequent visits. I've driven up from New York. I've just passed Capitol and Laurel. There is a huge highway system there now. They've been building it for some years. At that intersection there used to be a drugstore – Childs. Another of my crimes was to run up a charge account there. Hershey bars and licorice sticks. As my capacity was infinite, this finally had to be stopped. I can eat a pound of chocolates with joy – thanks to Childs Drugstore. Training *is* important.

Well, if you go up Laurel to Capitol and over the railroad bridge – corner of Laurel and Hawthorn (on our right) – there used to be Murphy's Grocery and Butcher Shop. The building is still there. Fig newtons – fly biscuits – and a poisonous concoction of chocolate and marshmallow on a vanilla cookie (so fine for the teeth and digestion that they stopped making it). Yes, Mr Murphy, wherever you are, I remember you well. Those square tin boxes with the glass fronts so that you could see and taste, not the packaged stalies of today. And Mr Murphy let us sample.

Well, we must leave Murphy's and turn left or west on Hawthorn to what used to be 133. First the factory, the Arrow Electric Company, then the edge of our front lawn is still there. The driveway.

Our house is gone – Victorian gothic – three gables, trimmed with black lace. The driveway – the trees – gracious, simple – the brook – the daffodils. Gone. Even the brook has been put into a pipe. Well, that's the style today – pipe things – can things – freeze things – computerize things. Have to be careful about that. You can't develop a mind full of beauty or tender imagination and independence of spirit tearing along in a box without a bit of space and air – number XY-133-609-00. Well, yes, there are indeed so many of us and we've got to make room.

Anyway, they saved the north end of Nook Farm. This includes the north end of Forest Street. Mark Twain's house and the Harriet Beecher Stowe house. My sister Marion was involved in this. What a great job has been done in restoring them! And although it is a generation before, it is the same atmosphere that I was brought up in. The matting-covered floors upstairs. The style of fireplace – the slate and marbleized mantels – the kitchen – the windows bayed to catch the sun. Cozy places to sit. It is full of ideas for living and enjoying. Go and see it. All the details. They've done it so carefully. The carpets and lack of window curtains on the south side. Harriet Beecher Stowe's flower paintings. The furniture she painted. The garden: she grew tomatoes and geraniums side by side. Oh, *geraniums*!

As I told you, when I was a kid I drove all over Hartford to my various lessons. No license, of course. Well, I was turning off Asylum south onto Prospect. The corner of Elizabeth Park. I was stopped by a ditchdigger. We had waved at each other and smiled when I passed every morning – so I stopped the car and he came over and presented me with a big box of candy. I was thrilled. Off I went. And that night at dinner I told Dad and Mother about it. Dad was furious.

'You must give it back.'

 'Oh, but I've eaten half of –'

'You must give it back. You must not stop.'

Well, I wasn't about to return a half-eaten box – I just changed my route.

Do you realize that in those days Asylum went only as far as Steele Road, then it was a path – through sort of bushes – trees – you know – really a dirt path? And as little girls we were warned about walking there because men would lurk and sometimes expose themselves – imagine!

'And what would you do?' I asked a friend who told me about how it happened to her. 'What did you do?' I asked.

'What do you suppose I did? I looked. That was what he wanted, wasn't it?'

'Well, yes, I suppose it was,' I answered.

And now I always smile as I drive out Asylum past Steele Road. Well, you laugh about it, but indeed – it was what he wanted.

Isn't it funny? Hartford is two places to me: it's what it was and it is what it is. I'll come back and find out all about that, but in the meantime I have a view, then I skip how many years and there's the present.

Connecticut. Aren't we lucky? We have wonderful wildflowers – parks – hills – lovely old houses.

We have a pace that we like – sometimes slow – sometimes fast. Rivers – reservoirs – Long Island Sound. A wonderful climate – trees – gardens – snow – rain. And it's a good size – not huge – not small.

Well, it's home to me. I've been stuck in the snow. I've lost a house in a hurricane. I've tennised. I've golfed. It's been fun. I've lived there and I'll be buried there.

I was married to Luddy there on December 12, 1928. Grandfather Hepburn officiated. Marion and Ellsworth were married there – a big wedding. Peg and I were bridesmaids. Dad and Mother both died there. Mother in 1951 – Dad in 1962. Santa (Dad's second wife, Madeline Santa Croce) was lonely in such a big house by herself. She moved into her sister's apartment.

Dad was really the last inhabitant of the Hartford house.

After Mother's death, he married Santa. She was one of his nurses. I had always felt that Dad married Santa because he didn't want any of his children to feel that they were responsible for him. It worked. Santa had always been in love with him, and she was thrilled with the idea. He gave her a wonderful life – full of adventure and study. They had fascinating trips to Greece and Egypt. I went with them twice. Frances Rich, my California friend, went with us once – it was fun. Then Dad got sick.

In 1960–61–62, Dad began to feel rotten. Santa took good care of him, and at a certain period when it got to be a bit too much for her, Phyllis, my secretary, went to help.

I remember having a long conversation with my brother Bob on the telephone about Dad. I was on the West Coast with Spencer at this time, so that I was not really up on Dad's situation. Dad would never complain about how he felt. He simply *would not* say that he was suffering. Actually, Bob said that he must have been in a terrible state. They discovered that he had a burst gall bladder. It had been full of stones and of course his abdomen was full of stones and of bile too. Hard as a rock. He was gradually being poisoned. Bob said that the pain must have been really excruciating – not a word from Dad. He found moaning about one's health totally disgusting. He was operated on by Dr Welles Standish. His blood pressure went down too far and it finally affected his ability to think and to talk. He had to then have a prostate operation. Bob did this operation. It wasn't customary to operate on a close relative but Bob thought that he could do it best. It was his specialty. So he did it. Bob said Dad at this time acted as though he were quietly studying his own demise – never a word of complaint. He just endured or he'd catch Bob's eye and would smile or wink at him.

I got back to Hartford for a little visit. Dad had moved down to the first floor, to the study, which luckily had a bathroom off it. He seemed happy, as always, but much weaker.

One morning Bob and I were eating breakfast in the dining room across the hall. We went in to see how Dad was and he seemed to be just quietly leaving this world. He smiled – he looked at us and he slowly stopped breathing. His chin fell. He closed his eyes – he was gone – just gone. Bob and I sat there. Such a remarkable man Dad had been. So strong. So definite. So tough and funny. He'll never be forgotten.

As Bob told the story, he would stop – really overcome with emotion. His memory was vivid – Dad's tolerance of pain was unbelievable.

Such a powerhouse coming to the end of the trail.

He was eighty-odd. He wrote his own rules – and followed them to the smallest detail – 'Row your own boat.'

What wonderful examples our parents! Oh – we were so lucky.

Santa stayed for several years – and it was then that she decided to move in with her sister. The house was lonely and just too big for one woman. She told us what she wanted.

Bob didn't want to live there. Peg couldn't – I couldn't – Dick was in Fenwick.

So it was over – life at 201. Clean it up – move out – and give it to Hartford University.

The moving out was quite a job, a very very sad job for all of us – it was the end of our beginning.

Bryn Mawr

I went to Bryn Mawr College. I was in the class of 1928. My first year I lived in a suite – room and bedroom, ground floor, first door on the right. Pembroke West. There was also a Pembroke East, and between the two was a gateway and over it a huge dining room. My friends from Ethel Walker lived in another hall – Merion. Having not been in school for several years, I was really not at home or at ease with a lot of strange girls. I used to go to bed very early. Then I'd get up at four or four-thirty and I'd go down the hall to the bathroom and have solitude in the hot and cold showers and in the john. I used to eat fruit and cereal and milk for breakfast, so I could have that alone in my room and avoid too many girls. Actually, I finally avoided the dining room altogether. In the early part of the semester I had gone into the dining room and started for the Pem West table. I was dressed in a French blue flared skirt which buttoned up the front with big white buttons – and an Iceland blue-and-white sweater popular at the time. I certainly did not consider myself beautiful. I was just painfully self-conscious. To my horror, I heard a voice – a New York voice – from the vicinity of where I was supposed to sit: 'Self-conscious Beauty!'

I nearly dropped dead. God knows I didn't consider myself a beauty. Oh dear. No. I continued into the room. I sat. I ate food. That year I never went back into that dining room.

I used to eat with my friends over in Merion, or I'd buy myself dinner at the College Inn. Dad gave me seventy-five dollars a month and food wasn't so expensive then.

I went to Europe for the first time with my friend Alice Palache the summer of our freshman year – 1925. I had $500 – she had $750. We were going to bicycle around England – but when we got off the boat and went to London on the train, we were horrified at the hills and small mountains, so we decided that we would buy a car and spend the night either in the car or on the ground or on a haystack to make up the expense. The agony of this for Palache was that she liked coffee in the morning. I didn't yet drink coffee – so I was fine with fruit and cold cereal and milk. What I missed most was the hot bath and the cold shower.

Sometimes we'd go in for a meal and go to 'wash our hands,' and if there was a tub I'd tear off my clothes and squat down in the tub and take a quick spray from the taps. I always traveled with a towel handy. It was fun. We went all over England, to Wales and to Scotland. When we got back to London, we sold the car for more than we'd paid for it, which was certainly lucky.

We then went to Paris – stayed at the Cayré Hotel on the Boulevard Raspail. There was a little restaurant across the street and we ate there most of the time. We had a table next to a long wall mirror and Palache had a fit because she said that I kept studying myself and my expression while we sat there.

We really went all over the city – which was of course thrilling – and went home penniless.

And my second year I roomed with a girl I'd gotten to know and so it wasn't so bad. Anyway, I'd gotten used to all the girls and I suppose they'd gotten used to me. I belonged to a particular group. Easier to function with the protection of a few others. These have more or less remained my friends, especially the ones living in New York or Connecticut. My last three years at Bryn Mawr were nowhere near as traumatic. I wasn't a member of any club but I acted in several plays, which was fun – and fooled around with my pals and laughed a lot. One of my friends had a car (Lib Rhett). Oh, what a treat! We went everywhere.

I played the leading man in one play – *The Truth About Blayds*, by A. A. Milne. I played the juvenile. I had to wear a wig covering my long hair. And a pair of pants a bit tight in the seat. It was a modern play. I remember one frightful moment when we were giving a performance of it at the Colony Club in New York. Somehow or other I managed to put my hand in my pants pocket and then to sit down. After a bit I tried to get my hand out of the pocket. Impossible. I tried several times. I got a bit confused and kept yanking. This turned out to be a splendid laugh.

I also played Teresa in *The Cradle Song*, by Martínez Sierra.

In my last year I played Pandora in John Lyly's *The Woman in the Moon*. This was part of a big May Day production. It was done in the cloister of the library with the sun full on our faces. The play had not been done ever in this country, and a lot of very highbrow interest was shown.

I think I was chosen for the part by Samuel Arthur King. Dr King gave a course in speech, which was a required course. It interested me a great deal. He had been hired by M. Carey Thomas, former head of Bryn Mawr, who was very conscious of American speech and its unfortunate production. Mother and Dad were also very voice-conscious and reminded us often that it was more attractive to make an attractive sound.

Pandora was a great part. She played in different moods under the influence of different planets. I was warlike under Mars. Loving under Venus, etc., etc. Funny, tearful, etc. My father said that all he could see in that performance were the soles of my dirty feet getting blacker and blacker. And my freckled face getting redder and redder.

When I was at Bryn Mawr, they didn't allow smoking except in the smoking room, first floor. I lived in Pembroke East at the time, on the second floor just outside the dining room which was the sort of bridge between Pembroke East and Pembroke West. This was my senior year – 1927–8. I had just picked up my mail and was going through it. The door of my room was opened into the hall.

'Heavens – what is this?' A small package. I tore off the wrapping – a box of perfumed cigarettes.

'Oh, a good smell – I think I'll try one.' I put one of the cigarettes in my mouth – lit it and puffed away.

'Oh, a bit weird. Well, that's that.' Put it out – threw it away.

Later that day a student-government officer said to me, 'You were smoking in your room. Someone reported you. It's against the rules.'

I looked and was dumbfounded. 'Who reported me?'

'I can't tell you.'

'Oh – I see. Yes – well . . .'

Now the truth of the matter was that I was not a smoker, so I didn't know any of the smoking regulations. Obviously, someone passing my door had seen me smoking that perfumed cigarette. It must have been someone who didn't like me – otherwise she would have yelled at me, 'Hey, what are you *doing*?'

I couldn't say that I didn't smoke. It would put whoever it was in a very difficult position.

You can see by these letters that I was suspended

for eight days. Never could tell anyone I didn't smoke. So – an eight-day holiday.

October 20, 1927

My dear Dr Hepburn,

The copy of a letter to Miss Hepburn which I enclose will explain itself.

This particular regulation would be made by anyone who had charge of the college and its enforcement would always be imperative. I am sorry that after living in a community for three years your daughter did not feel responsible herself in such matters and that the community had to take it in hand.

Very sincerely yours,

(Signed) Marion Edwards Park

Dr Thomas N. Hepburn

October 20th, 1927

My dear Miss Hepburn,

In view of your failure to keep the regulation which forbids a student to smoke in her college room, the Bryn Mawr Association of Self Government has asked me to notify you of your suspension from the college halls and from all college exercises from Sunday October 23rd at noon to the evening of Friday October 28th. Your absences from classes during the week will be regarded by the college as though they were unexcused cuts.

I am sorry that you have disregarded a restriction

which has been established as a matter of common agreement among the students and which, dealing as it does with conditions in large buildings filled with casual people and inflammable things, must have the support of your own common sense if you give it thought.

I am sending a copy of this letter to your father in order that he may understand your return home at this time.

Sincerely yours,

(Signed) Marion Edwards Park

Miss Katharine Hepburn
Pembroke West

October 22, 1927

My dear President Park,

I am naturally much concerned that my daughter Katharine has been deprived for five days of her opportunity to work, as she has already had to miss several days because of the wedding of her best friend. It is perfectly possible that this additional handicap may endanger the successful completion of her year's work, necessary for her degree. While such a punishment may be deserved by the enormity of the crime committed, I, who am deeply interested in my daughter's successful work, naturally turn to an analysis of the crime. This crime is 'smoking in her room at college'.

I note that there is a regulation against students smoking in their rooms, 'established by a common agreement among the students'. In other words it is technically a regulation inspired by the reasoned conviction of a self governing body. I note in your personal letter that you say 'This particular regulation would be made by anyone who had charge of the college'. Such being the case, it is hardly a voluntary regulation of the self governing student body, except in a technical sense.

The reasons given for the regulation are 'conditions in large buildings filled with casual people and inflammable things'. In support of the validity of these reasons you appeal to 'her common sense if she will give it thought'.

I would suggest, however, that in so far as you educate these girls and then appeal to their 'common sense' and 'thought', it would be well to see whether the reasons given for the rule against smoking in their rooms would stand the test of such an appeal. If they do not, the college has, just so far, lost its educational authority.

In Katharine's experience both her parents smoke. They smoke in their rooms if they wish – and, funny as it may seem, Katharine rarely smokes, altho no home restrictions have been put on her.

Katharine has never been in a hotel or business office or even large hospital where smoking has been prohibited, altho they were filled with many more 'casual people' and much more 'inflammable' material.

I feel, therefore, that the appeal to her common sense and thought is ill advised.

The one and only appeal in this case should be that she must obey the rules – however irrational those rules may seem to her.

I shall take such a position with her. I shall emphasize the absurdity of endangering her degree and negativing all the money I have spent on her education by breaking a rule in order to indulge a passing whim. To such an extent can I back up your discipline. I can not back it up as a regulation having a spontaneous origin in the student body, or a regulation appealing to her 'common sense' and 'thought'.

Very sincerely yours,
Thomas N. Hepburn

To President Marion Edwards Park

Before my senior year ended, I had made friends with a man named Jack Clarke, who lived in a house next door to the college campus. His best friend was Ludlow Ogden Smith.

Jack had several friends in the theatre and he happened to know Edwin Knopf, who ran a theater company – a very good one, with big stars – in Baltimore. Mary Boland, Kenneth MacKenna, Eliot Cabot. I got him to give me a letter to Knopf, and one weekend Lib Rhett and I drove over to Baltimore. My mother's sister Edith Houghton

Hooker lived there. I went to see Knopf and he said, 'Well, write me a note when you finish college.'

I finished college.

Dad always said if you want to get something, don't write. Don't telephone. Be there yourself. In person. Harder to turn down a living presence.

I thought, No – no note. I'll appear myself.

So I did. My aunt and her family had left Baltimore and gone to Maine for the summer, so I stayed at the Bryn Mawr Club. It, too, was half closed, but they let me stay in their cheaper room, in a hall bedroom. On an air shaft. High ceilings, very dark and scary. Not too far from the theatre. I was too shy to go into a restaurant. I'd hardly ever been in a restaurant, in fact. And certainly not alone. My great friend Bob McKnight, who had a car (you see how wise I was in picking friends), had come with me. He was on his way to Rome to study sculpture. He'd won a Prix de Rome. He lived there with me. And we'd get food from a delicatessen. It was all very innocent. We were both wildly ambitious and thrilled with life and its possibilities. We weren't wasting our strength rolling around. It was all or nothing for *me me me*. With each of us. Don't get sidetracked. We protected each other.

I went to see Eddie Knopf. I found my way in from the front. I didn't even know there was such a thing as a stage door. I heard voices. It sounded like a rehearsal. I opened a door so that I could see the stage. It was a rehearsal. I crept in and sat in a back row like a mouse. An hour passed. I needed to go to the bathroom. Finally, I *had* to go to the bathroom. The whole theatre away from the stage area was black as pitch. I felt my way around the lobby – down a stairway into another lobby. And finally a john. Then I found my way out and went back to my spot. Another hour. Even a third. Then all of a sudden it was over. They were finishing. The lights in the auditorium came on.

Eddie Knopf saw me. He walked up the aisle. Stopped by me and said, 'Oh – you – yes, report for rehearsal Monday – eleven o'clock.'

And he was gone.

My God! I had a job! He gave me a job! He knew me! He gave me a job!

That Monday I walked into his office at ten-forty-five.

'I'm here for rehearsal.'

'You're in the wrong place.'

It was thus I learned about the stage door.

I went in. It was quite a large group. The play was to be *The Czarina* – Mary Boland, the Czarina. The parts were handed around. 'Oh, mine is quite large – about ten pages.'

There were a number of young girls beside myself but I had the biggest part.

We were all introduced to one another. Then we sat around a big table and read the play. Thrilling! My part was really very nice. Wasn't I lucky!

The rehearsals were many and long. It was announced that the costumes would be assigned in the morning at eleven. I thought, Well, get there early. I got there at ten. I was not the first to arrive. I was the last. Well, that was a big shock. I wasn't as clever as I thought. And of course I got the worst costume. Inches too short and not very becoming in the neck.

Then something very strange happened. One of the girls came up to me and said, 'I was the first here. I want you to take my costume. It's the prettiest.'

I was struck dumb. I'd hardly spoken to the girl. I looked at her. She had the dress on. It was lovely. I tried to talk.

 'Oh, but I – but you – but oh no, I couldn't –'

She stopped me. 'I'm going to be married,' she said. 'I'm not going to be an actor. And I think that you are going to be. I mean, I think you are going to be a big star. I want you to have it.'

What could I say? Of course I said, 'Oh yes yes. Thank you – I mean thank you very – I mean – oh, how lovely – I'm so relieved – it's so – But you – you are an angel – you are the soul of generosity. I can't believe that you – Oh, please – Oh, I'm thunderstruck – I – No, don't stop me –'

She stopped me: 'Look, I'll take it off and you give me that and I'll give you this, and you'll be happy and I'll be happy.'

We changed clothes. I turned and looked in the mirror. Oh, perfection. 'Oh, I'm –' I turned back. She had gone.

Can you imagine anyone being that generous? Wasn't I lucky? Lucky. Do you think it will last? I got the best dress by far. And I don't even remember her name.

The play was about to open. I was totally ignorant of the ways of the theatre. I had no makeup and used no makeup except lipstick – Christy's No. 2, bright red-orange. Mary Boland told me what makeup to get. How to do eyes. I watched her make up. She was so generous. Gave me all sorts of bits and pieces.

They were all very nice to me, the stars of the company. The play opened. I got two very nice notices for my little part. I was known a bit socially in Baltimore, as I told you. I hoped that that wasn't the reason I was noticed. But, for whatever reason, the *Printed Word* said I was 'arresting'. And I was given a part in the next week's show, *The Torch Bearers.* This was another play which Mary Boland had done. There was a part for me, not a very good one. And I knew that I was not very good in it. When I got nervous, my voice would shoot up into the top of my head. I didn't really know how to control this. I talked to Kenneth MacKenna. He suggested that when I left the company I should go to New York and study voice with a woman named Frances Robinson-Duff. Ina Claire was one of her pupils. Duff was very well known.

'She's the best voice teacher in New York City.'

Well, why wait, I thought. I'll drop this and go to New York. I looked her up. Found out how much she charged.

My father had been disgusted and heartsick over the fact that I wanted to act. Thought it a silly profession closely allied to streetwalking. That I had developed into a cheap show-off and that I was entering a shabby profession which was based on youth and looks. Definitely a foundation of sand for a silly life. He wasn't about to be the financial backer of such a project. My mother was all for it. Anything I wanted just so I didn't settle for the old routine of nursemaid to the rising generation. She thought women should give life a whirl. See if they could swing it so that they could be more independent of the male sex. Dad was for this too. He just didn't care for the road I'd chosen.

But I'd saved up some allowance money and when I went to Baltimore I had over $250. A lot to me. But not enough for New York. And certainly not enough for Frances Robinson-Duff. So I wrote Dad a letter which I thought would sell him. The importance of training for the job I'd chosen. Would he back me? He had already sent me fifty dollars, which he said he had won on a golf match or a bridge game. Gambling money was not real money, so he was sending it on to me. After that, of course, I knew that with a small push he would be on my side. We were very close, Dad and Mother and I. None of us liked the separate ways. So, of course, he told me yes – he'd pay for Duff. And so I left Baltimore and away I went to New York City after the second week.

Aunt Betty Hepburn had an extra room in a brownstone in the East Sixties. She was the widow of Uncle Charles, Dad's brother.

Frances Robinson-Duff was an experience. A house on East Sixty-second – between Second and Third. She and her mother. Her mother had been an opera singer. She taught opera. Frances was tall – about five feet seven. She was stout – big stomach, medium bosom, corseted. Her office was the top floor. She sat and tried to teach me how to speak from my diaphragm. I would have to put my hand on her diaphragm and hold it there (my hand) as she pursed her lips to blow out a candle. It was a strange feeling. I had my hand on the top of a corset. It was somehow very embarrassing to me. Her bosom – her diaphragm – the top of that corset. I don't think that at that time I really got the notion of producing air from the diaphragm rather than straining the throat. Now I can call 'HEY!' straight from the diaphragm. But my lack of success with really connecting my voice and volume to the diaphragm cost me great worries in my career. I lost my voice and would get very hoarse whenever I played a part which was fast and loud. It was an agony.

Too bad that I was not able to really understand all of Duff's candle-blowing, etc., in the beginning. I would have saved myself great agony. In a way, I can understand why I couldn't connect voice and diaphragm. I think that I was so excited by life and living and my future that I was simply wound up so tight I didn't – couldn't – relax.

Frances Robinson-Duff was really interested in me. She did her very best and she helped me to learn my way around in the theatre. And I had Mother and Dad backing me all the way – Mother on the telephone, Dad with his letters.

Dear Kath,

Can't let your 21st birthday go by without a wee bit of sentimental indulgence. You are now a free lance and your Dad has no control over you. Just think of that! Doesn't it make you shudder when you think of the past 21 years of servitude. Just for that I now shall order you around as successfully in the future as in the past.

First, don't take life or its happenings too seriously. Lift up the corners of that mouth that I gave you one moonlight night.

Second, try to do one thing well – utilizing the experience of all preceding life and your own wit.

Third, never let yourself *hate* any person. It is the most devastating weapon of one's enemies.

Fourth, always remember that your Dad is liable to call you all sorts of names when he disapproves of your behavior, but don't take him too seriously, and always come to him – whatever your difficulty – he may be able to help you. Impossibly, he may not be as stupid as he looks.

Fifth, forget all the above and remember only that I would love to kiss you 21 times and give you a million dollars –

Your hopeless Dad

PENGUIN 60s

ISABEL ALLENDE · *Voices in My Ear*
NICHOLSON BAKER · *Playing Trombone*
LINDSEY BAREHAM · *The Little Book of Big Soups*
KAREN BLIXEN · *From the Ngong Hills*
DIRK BOGARDE · *Coming of Age*
ANTHONY BURGESS · *Childhood*
ANGELA CARTER · *Lizzie Borden*
CARLOS CASTANEDA · *The Sorcerer's Ring of Power*
ELIZABETH DAVID · *Peperonata and Other Italian Dishes*
RICHARD DAWKINS · *The Pocket Watchmaker*
GERALD DURRELL · *The Pageant of Fireflies*
RICHARD ELLMANN · *The Trial of Oscar Wilde*
EPICURUS · *Letter on Happiness*
MARIANNE FAITHFULL · *Year One*
KEITH FLOYD · *Hot and Spicy Floyd*
ALEXANDER FRATER · *Where the Dawn Comes Up Like Thunder*
ESTHER FREUD · *Meeting Bilal*
JOHN KENNETH GALBRAITH · *The Culture of Contentment*
ROB GRANT AND DOUG NAYLOR · *Scenes from the Dwarf*
ROBERT GRAVES · *The Gods of Olympus*
JANE GRIGSON · *Puddings*
SOPHIE GRIGSON · *From Sophie's Table*
KATHARINE HEPBURN · *Little Me*
SUSAN HILL · *The Badness Within Him*
ALAN HOLLINGHURST · *Adventures Underground*
BARRY HUMPHRIES · *Less is More Please*
HOWARD JACOBSON · *Expulsion from Paradise*
P. D. JAMES · *The Girl Who Loved Graveyards*
STEPHEN KING · *Umney's Last Case*
LAO TZU · *Tao Te Ching*
DAVID LEAVITT · *Chips Is Here*

PENGUIN 60S

LAURIE LEE · *To War in Spain*
PATRICK LEIGH FERMOR · *Loose as the Wind*
ELMORE LEONARD · *Trouble at Rindo's Station*
DAVID LODGE · *Surprised by Summer*
BERNARD MAC LAVERTY · *The Miraculous Candidate*
SHENA MACKAY · *Cloud-Cuckoo-Land*
NORMAN MAILER · *The Dressing Room*
PETER MAYLE · *Postcards from Summer*
JAN MORRIS · *Scenes from Havian Life*
BLAKE MORRISON · *Camp Cuba*
VLADIMIR NABOKOV · *Now Remember*
REDMOND O'HANLON · *A River in Borneo*
STEVEN PINKER · *Thinking in Tongues*
CRAIG RAINE · *Private View*
CLAUDIA RODEN · *Ful Medames and Other Vegetarian Dishes*
HELGE RUBINSTEIN · *Chocolate Parfait*
SIMON SCHAMA · *The Taking of the Bastille*
WILL SELF · *The Rock of Crack As Big As the Ritz*
MARK SHAND · *Elephant Tales*
NIGEL SLATER · *30-Minute Suppers*
RICK STEIN · *Fresh from the Sea*
LYTTON STRACHEY · *Florence Nightingale*
PAUL THEROUX · *Slow Trains to Simla*
COLIN THUBRON · *Samarkand*
MARK TULLY · *Beyond Purdah*
LAURENS VAN DER POST · *Merry Christmas, Mr Lawrence*
MARGARET VISSER · *More than Meets the Eye*
GAVIN YOUNG · *Something of Samoa*

and

Thirty Obituaries from Wisden · SELECTED BY MATTHEW ENGEL

READ MORE IN PENGUIN

For complete information about books available from Penguin and how to order them, please write to us at the appropriate address below. Please note that for copyright reasons the selection of books varies from country to country.